RAND

PACE-FORWARD

Policy Analytic and Computational Environment for Dutch Freight Transport

Manuel J. Carrillo

with Richard J. Hillestad, Patricia G.J. Twaalfhoven, Joseph G. Bolten, Odette A.W.T. van de Riet, Warren E. Walker

Supported by the
Netherlands Ministry of Transport,
Public Works and Water Management

European-American Center for Policy Analysis

Preface

To aid the Freight Options for Road, Waterway, and Rail for the Dutch (FORWARD) study, a decision support system (DSS) was designed and developed for use in analyzing freight transport policies. The design and capabilities of that system—Policy Analytic and Computational Environment for Dutch Freight Transport (PACE-FORWARD)—are described in this report.

The FORWARD study was performed by RAND's European-American Center for Policy Analysis (EAC), in cooperation with the School of Systems Engineering, Policy Analysis, and Management of the Delft University of Technology, on behalf of the Dutch Ministry of Transport, Public Works, and Water Management. The study examined the benefits and costs of various proposed changes (called tactics) to the Dutch system of freight transport, and developed strategies for mitigating the adverse impacts of the expected growth in road freight transport while retaining the economic benefits. A detailed description of the study's approach and results is contained in the main report for the study: *FORWARD—Freight Options for Road, Water, and Rail for the Dutch: Final Report*, MR-736-EAC/VW, RAND, 1996, by Richard J. Hillestad, Warren E. Walker, Manuel J. Carrillo, Joseph G. Bolten, Patricia G.J. Twaalfhoven, and Odette A.W.T. van de Riet. An executive summary of the main report is given in *FORWARD—Freight Options for Road, Water, and Rail for the Dutch: Executive Summary*, MR-739-EAC/VW, RAND, 1996, by Richard J. Hillestad, Warren E. Walker, Manuel J. Carrillo, Joseph G. Bolten, Patricia G.J. Twaalfhoven, and Odette A.W.T. van de Riet.

PACE-FORWARD offers a spreadsheet environment containing tools and models to support policy analysis, including models for air-pollutant emissions, safety, noise, congestion, cost, and macroeconomic impacts. As a DSS, PACE-FORWARD has integrated data and model bases and a graphical user interface. Because of these two aspects of PACE-FORWARD, this report should be of interest to both policy analysts and DSS designers.

The EAC, an independently chartered European unit of RAND, is located in Delft, the Netherlands. It operates as a foundation (Stichting), chartered in The Hague under Dutch law. The mission of the EAC is to conduct interdisciplinary analyses of public policy problems facing Europe and North America; to convey the results of these analyses to the policymaking community, the research community, and the public at large; and to foster cooperation among researchers in all parts of Europe and North America. The EAC seeks to accomplish its mission through research projects of interest to governments and society as a whole. EAC research is conducted alone, in conjunction with individuals and research organizations in the Netherlands and throughout Europe, and through close cooperation with other RAND sites.

For more information about PACE-FORWARD, please contact

Dr. Manuel J. Carrillo
RAND
P.O. Box 2138
Santa Monica, CA 90407-2138
U.S.A.
Tel: +1-310-393-0411, Ext. 6662
E-mail: carrillo@rand.org

or

Dr. Warren E. Walker
European-American Center for Policy Analysis
c/o TU Delft
Landbergstraat 6
2628 CE Delft, The Netherlands
Tel: +31-15-2785411
E-mail: warrenw@sepa.tudelft.nl

Contents

Figures

Tables

Summary

Freight transport is an economic area in which Dutch companies have a large stake, not just nationally but internationally as well. Consistent with various economic expansion plans, the Dutch government expects substantial growth in Dutch freight transport between now and 2010. For example, between 1986 and 2010, international transport loaded or unloaded in the Netherlands is expected to double.

Understandably, the Dutch government is trying to be prepared, given that growth in freight transport can have adverse environmental and other effects as well as economic benefits. As part of this preparation, the Dutch Ministry of Transport, Public Works, and Water Management asked the European-American Center for Policy Analysis (EAC) to help screen and assess numerous options, or tactics, aimed at mitigating the adverse effects of freight transport growth while allowing its economic benefits. This effort became known as the Freight Options for Road, Water, and Rail for the Dutch (FORWARD) study.

The scope of the FORWARD study was quite broad. The Netherlands uses many modes of freight transport, three of which were considered: road, inland waterway, and rail. Furthermore, the types of tactics were quite varied, ranging from transport efficiency (e.g., higher utilization of capacity for freight transport), to modal shift, to direct mitigation (e.g., use of a cleaner-emission truck engine).

Given the wide spectrum of environmental impacts associated with transport, the EAC developed a conceptual, logical framework within which to assess these transport tactics for three projected economic and freight transport scenarios. This framework made use of cost and macroeconomic models, as well as engineering models for air-pollutant emissions, safety, noise, and congestion. Some of these models were in existence, others had to be designed from scratch. In all cases, the models had to be integrated into an analytic environment in which they could be used with consistent data and could use each other's intermediate results. This integration of models and data into a computer-based spreadsheet environment for use in the FORWARD policy analysis led to what became known as the Policy Analytic and Computational Environment for Dutch Freight Transport, or PACE-FORWARD.

The PACE-FORWARD design and the challenges involved in PACE-FORWARD's development may be seen from two different perspectives.

Viewed as a (computer) decision support system (DSS), the Excel spreadsheet environment is useful in integrating PACE-FORWARD's model bases and data bases, its graphical user interface, and their respective management systems and control programs. Some of the challenges related to DSS design and development were

- The difficulty of dealing with many spreadsheet models.
- Limitations in the spreadsheet environment caused mainly by the rather basic data base management system capabilities of Excel version 4 (the latest Macintosh version available during the study).
- How to achieve model and data consistency in integrating the many models.

Viewed from the perspective of policy analysis (and, in part, modeling), some typical issues were

- What models to use.
- What level of resolution to use so that the models representing the transport system would capture the contributions of the tactics.
- How to assure that the models adequately represented the transport tactics.
- How to translate scenarios into model inputs.
- What performance measures to compute.
- What tools to have the DSS provide in order to facilitate tactic comparison and screening and the generation of strategies (combinations of tactics).

These and other problems and issues had to be dealt with within the limited time and resources of the FORWARD study.

PACE-FORWARD's complementary models (emissions, costs, etc.) provide a rich set of performance measures (many displayed in graphs); additional measures can be added through PACE-FORWARD's accessible spreadsheet environment. These measures can be used to compare tactics and, for a given tactic, to find out the relative contributions of some subset of the transport sector. For example, for a selected tactic, analysts can compute the relative contributions to air-pollutant emissions of the following:

- Road versus rail versus inland waterway transport
- Freight versus passenger transport
- National versus international transport

And within these categories, they can further see the relative contributions by

- Geographic region
- Commodity class

The performance measures provide the visibility needed in regional and national planning to enable stakeholders to understand how proposals will affect their specific areas of concern.

PACE-FORWARD provided an adequate logical and conceptual framework for the FORWARD study. It also provided the capability needed to assess the numerous transport tactics considered, which helped in screening out tactics that held no promise so that the focus could shift to a smaller set of tactics for more careful study.

Acknowledgments

Many individuals shared with us their expertise on the Dutch transport system. They included people from various agencies of the Dutch government, Dutch firms, the School of Systems Engineering, Policy Analysis, and Management at Delft University of Technology, RAND, and the EAC. The help they provided is gratefully acknowledged.

At the Dutch Ministry of Transport, Public Works, and Water Management, Paul van der Gaag and Max Klok, our project monitors, facilitated our access to some of the data that PACE-FORWARD requires for transport tactic assessment. Hans van der Rest provided helpful technical comments on PACE-FORWARD, and Joe Bekkers furnished data that proved to be very useful.

John Klein of the Dutch Central Bureau of Statistics provided clarification on the TNO (Netherlands Organization for Applied Scientific Research) truck emission models. Peter Blok and others at the Dutch firm NEI (Netherlands Economic Institute) shared their insights on costing, which helped with both the cost and macroeconomic models.

At RAND, James Stucker provided useful insights on what was to become the macroeconomic impact model; Dan Relles provided the statistical expertise in deriving the congestion model; and Judy Fischer provided valuable help in implementing the database management system extensions for data analysis. At the EAC, Henk Kloosterhuis helped collect data on the networks for the three modes of transport.

In all cases, any errors or omissions herein remain our own.

1. Introduction

The Dutch government, through its Central Planning Bureau (CPB), has been considering various economic scenarios projected for the year 2015. When these scenarios are translated into freight transport flows, they forecast that international freight transport—loaded or unloaded in the Netherlands—will double between 1986 and 2010. Because growth in freight transport can have adverse impacts on the environment, the Dutch Ministry of Transport, Public Works, and Water Management (hereinafter referred to as the Ministry) chose to sponsor a policy analysis of freight transport options—called tactics or, when combined, strategies—aimed at mitigating those effects while retaining the economic benefits. The Ministry then requested that the European-American Center for Policy Analysis (EAC) perform such an analysis, which later became known as the Freight Options for Road, Water, and Rail for the Dutch (FORWARD) study.

A policy analysis of freight transport options covers many areas, from the various types of environmental and economic impacts of a multimodal transport system to international issues. To estimate the impacts, analysts rely on objective models and other tools when available, and on subjective evaluation otherwise. For some areas, models may not be possible because the relationships among the component parts of what is being modeled may not be known. When models are possible, however, they can provide a logical and conceptual framework that captures the essential relationships. In any case, policy analysis requires the integration of facts, model results, and educated judgment to compare alternative options.

By their very nature, policy analyses in a given area are not performed on an ongoing basis but, instead, at the onset of a major project or when a problem of sufficient magnitude is perceived. This means that there may be problems at any one time with the existing models: they may cover only narrow, specialized areas; the data they use may not be current; they may be inconsistent with one another or unintegrated; etc. Therefore, when a policy analysis begins, the analysts need to immediately take stock of the state-of-the-art in modeling in the areas of interest, deciding which existing models can be used and whether it is feasible to embark on new modeling efforts. If new modeling must be done, the analysts must decide how extensive it is to be, always keeping in mind that not only does the modeling itself take time and other resources, but so does the gathering of the data that the model(s) will use.

When the Ministry requested that the EAC perform a policy analysis of options for Dutch freight transport, a search for models and analysis tools began. What that search led to was the design and use of a spreadsheet environment to assess over one hundred tactics that might mitigate the adverse effects of the projected growth in freight transport envisioned for three economic scenarios for the year 2015.[1] As designed, this system—Policy Analytic and Computational Environment for Dutch Freight Transport (PACE-FORWARD)—also provides a medium through which the conceptual framework of the analysis becomes apparent to PACE-FORWARD's users.

After looking into existing models of freight transport and judging what areas were amenable to modeling, PACE-FORWARD was developed to incorporate models in air-pollutant emissions, safety, noise, congestion, cost, and macroeconomic impacts. To handle the detailed data required by the numerous transport tactics being considered, existing models had to be adapted or enhanced and new models had to be built. Because all of these models were to be integrated into an analytic environment, each one had to be implemented in this consistent environment.

PACE-FORWARD is a decision support system (DSS) with the data base and model base necessary to perform policy analysis of Dutch freight transport options.[2] The integration of models and data and the environment's amenability to use by various analysts are typical requirements of a DSS. A major challenge in developing PACE-FORWARD was the wide scope of the policy analysis and the relatively short period of time allotted for the study's completion. The analysis covered over one hundred freight transport tactics (freight transport is a major sector of the Dutch economy) at the regional and national level for three projected economic and transport scenarios for three transport modes—road, rail, and inland waterway.[3] The actual period for research and development in the FORWARD study was about one and one-half years.

---

[1]The three scenarios are called balanced growth (significant growth), European renaissance (moderate growth), and global shift (little growth). These were originally developed by the Dutch CPB (1992).

[2]For a discussion of decision support systems, see Turban, 1988. Turban uses the terms *data base* and *model base* to cover, respectively, all the data and all the models of a DSS. He uses *data base management system* and *model base management system* correspondingly (see Section 3 herein). Here, we use the term *database* (one word) to refer to a closely related set of data usually stored under a common entity, such as a table or a file; thus, the *data base* may include many *databases*. And, in keeping with common usage in the database field, we use the term *database management system* rather than *data base management system*.

[3]Note that sea shipping was excluded.

This document describes PACE-FORWARD from two perspectives. It discusses what went into designing the PACE-FORWARD DSS, including its models and their integration and the selection of a spreadsheet environment for its development. In addition, this document describes how the DSS was tailored for policy analysis of Dutch freight transport options at the national level, including the choice of scenarios, the categorization of tactics, and, more importantly, how these were represented and assessed in the various DSS models.

Section 2 starts with the policy analysis problem faced by the FORWARD study and how it led to consideration of an analytic and computational environment. Section 3 describes this environment in DSS terminology. There, an overview of the DSS is given, as well as a sampling of the DSS's graphical user interface and data analysis capabilities.

Section 4 is an overview of the data and model bases and their integration. Sections 5 through 10 describe in turn the six individual impact models, touching again on the policy analysis problem, especially with respect to the representation of tactics in the DSS models. Section 11 discusses the contribution of PACE-FORWARD from the viewpoints of policy analysis and DSSs.

Finally, the Appendix presents statistics that give a sense of the magnitude and speed of the computer implementation.

2. Policy Analysis of Freight Transport

The Ministry has over the years sponsored studies that estimate the impacts of the projected growth of freight transport by the years 2010–2015. One such study projects that between 1986 and 2010, the growth rate in the number of tonnes transported will be about 1.6 and 3.1 percent per year, respectively, for national and international freight. What this means is that between 1986 and 2010, tonnage for national and international transport will have grown, respectively, by 50 and 100 percent (NEA, 1992b).

Such expected growth, though beneficial from the point of view of economic growth, will have adverse environmental and other impacts. The Ministry is therefore looking into tactics and strategies (combinations of tactics) that when implemented will mitigate these adverse impacts (for example, the full-scale use of truck engines that are environmentally cleaner than those currently used). Many tactics have been proposed by the Dutch government and others; the Ministry is trying to identify those of potential for additional study and possible inclusion in strategies for implementation.

The FORWARD Study

In view of the expected freight transport growth and its potential for adverse effects, the Ministry asked the EAC to perform an initial assessment and screening of tactics affecting freight transport. This effort became known as the FORWARD study.

The Ministry, Dutch stakeholders, and RAND/EAC research staff identified over one hundred tactics for assessment, and the EAC set out to assess them in an analytic framework. Some of the tactics considered have economic, environmental, and political dimensions, in both the domestic and the international arenas. It thus became clear that the tactic assessment would have to be a multidisciplinary effort and that the task of measuring and modeling some of the areas would be very difficult. From the start, analysis of the political and implementation issues associated with the tactics was left out of the FORWARD study, postponed for a subsequent study covering a smaller, screened set of tactics.

Given that existing economic and environmental goals are typically in conflict, tactic assessment requires multiple-criteria decision making. Although the FORWARD study's results include a ranking of tactics on a cost-effectiveness basis (that incorporates stakeholder priorities), one of the study's main contributions is the separate, consistent cost and environmental impact measures for each of the tactics. An executive can make decisions based on these separate impacts and on his or her own assessment of other areas not considered by the study.

Previous studies sponsored by the Dutch government led to the development of three scenarios for the year 2015 for each of the relevant modes of transport: road, rail, and inland waterway. These transport scenarios are based on three long-term economic scenarios provided by the Dutch CPB (1992): balanced growth, European renaissance, and global shift. The impacts of proposed tactics could certainly be measured in the world envisioned by each of these three scenarios; however, at the request of the study sponsors, the FORWARD study used mainly the European renaissance scenario.

In a policy analysis of freight transport options, models should be used whenever possible because they provide a rational way to assess and compare alternatives. An initial investigation to determine what models and methodologies could be used concluded that the existing model implementations were inadequate for FORWARD study purposes for various reasons:[1]

- Unavailable or unaffordable (i.e., proprietary).
- Too narrowly focused.
- Inadequately documented (e.g., black boxes).
- Unsuitable for assessing numerous tactics.
- Difficult to integrate in an overall assessment scheme.

We thus could not use the existing model implementations. We did, however, use some of the existing methodology within expanded models. These were integrated in a new logical framework, implemented on spreadsheets, that became PACE-FORWARD.

---

[1]See Tavasszy, 1994, for a review of existing freight transport models.

Approach to Tactic Assessment

To facilitate tactic analysis, we set out to design and build a logical framework of data and models that would translate a large amount of information pertaining to a tactic and turn it into a set of organized impact measures. The resulting analysis environment was named PACE-FORWARD.

The tactics all have costs and benefits. We defined costs to include accounting and financial costs; benefits could include impact measures in the environmental areas of air-pollutant emissions, safety, noise, and congestion.

In the economic area, standard costing methodology can be considered, especially for relating or comparing data to those of previous studies connected with any given tactic. Previous studies also point out what costing data were used and accepted in obtaining cost projections.

In the environmental areas, existing engineering models that usually represent a narrow area need to be used to adequately capture the environmental impacts, especially those that depend on new technologies.

The approach followed in the FORWARD study for tactic assessment was to build and then use an analysis environment with logical and mutually consistent models that provide tactic impact measures for later use in tactic comparisons. This environment, PACE-FORWARD, is a spreadsheet-based DSS that integrates impact models and their data and displays output impact measures in a graphical form: it is well suited for tactic analysis, comparison, and screening.

A Decision Support System for Policy Analysis

Computer-based DSSs have been applied to a variety of business decisions with varying degrees of success (see, for example, Turban, 1988). A DSS can provide a user-friendly environment in which embedded models and data provide assessments that can support—but not replace—the decision-making process. DSS models have limited scope, so gaps in coverage are bound to exist for the areas being modeled. Therefore, an analyst or decision maker needs to complement the results provided by a DSS with perspective and judgment regarding facets of the problem not adequately covered in the DSS.

In the case of PACE-FORWARD, the DSS includes models in the areas of air-pollutant emissions, safety, noise, congestion, cost, and macroeconomic impacts. This DSS also includes policy analysis tools such as those of what-if and sensitivity analysis: these may be used in suggesting new tactics or bounding the impact measure achieved by any one tactic. Although the DSS's functionality as a set of tools for assessment was more important to the FORWARD study than its graphical user interface, the DSS has proved surprisingly user-friendly and is being used by analysts both in the United States and in the Netherlands.

3. The PACE-FORWARD Decision Support System

The FORWARD study required models and supporting data to evaluate the transport tactics. The initial spreadsheet models implemented for this purpose quickly evolved into a DSS for strategic planning. For brevity of exposition, terminology related to the DSS field is used here to describe PACE-FORWARD. More detailed descriptions of the models used in the DSS are in subsequent sections.

Overview of the System

Figure 3.1 gives an overview of the PACE-FORWARD DSS. The DSS includes models and related impact measures for air-pollutant emissions, safety, noise, congestion, cost, and macroeconomic effects. Collectively, these models constitute the model base, and they are accessed and used in the DSS by a set of programs known as the model base management system. All the components of

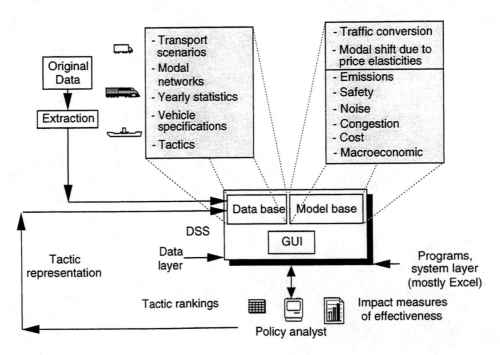

Figure 3.1—PACE-FORWARD as a Decision Support System

the DSS, including the programs of its management systems, are orchestrated by top-level control programs.

Analogous to the model base and its management system, the DSS also has a data base and its corresponding management system. Construction of the data base required the process known as data extraction, in which data are gathered or extracted from external data systems or other sources, such as printed documents. In the case of PACE-FORWARD, data source identification and extraction were a very extensive process.

Figure 3.1 shows some of the contents of the data base. In particular, it includes policy analytic data such as scenarios and tactics. Many times, data either were not readily available or had to be estimated based on previous studies or technical papers describing a new technology.

The other major component of the DSS is the graphical user interface (GUI), which facilitates DSS use and user-DSS communication. The GUI may include a control panel, menus, dialog boxes, or other graphical controls and displays. The DSS's ease of use resulted in part from using standard menus and dialogs familiar to users of Macintosh computers or Microsoft Windows programs. As with the data base and model base, the GUI also has a set of programs that implements it.

PACE-FORWARD was implemented on Excel version 4 (Microsoft Corporation, 1992), which was the latest Excel software available for Macintosh computers at the time of the study.[1] Excel then took on the role of the "DSS generator," which includes Excel's macro language and functions that provide and control the GUI, that perform basic database functions, and that implement models. Major factors in the decision to use Excel were the availability of mathematical functions and the ability to add compiled-language functions, the accessibility to the data in spreadsheets, the graphics capability, and the DSS portability to U.S. and Dutch RAND/EAC offices and, potentially, to the Ministry. (More on the selection of the Excel environment is in Section 4.)

A Sampling of the Graphical User Interface

Figure 3.2 shows the PACE-FORWARD control panel, and Figure 3.3 shows the listing of functions available through its menus.

---

[1]With minor changes, the DSS could also function on a PC-type computer.

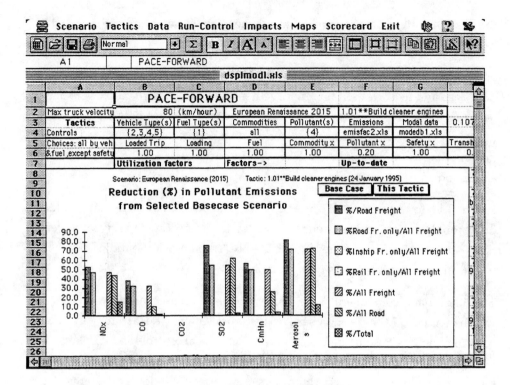

Figure 3.2—PACE-FORWARD's Control Panel

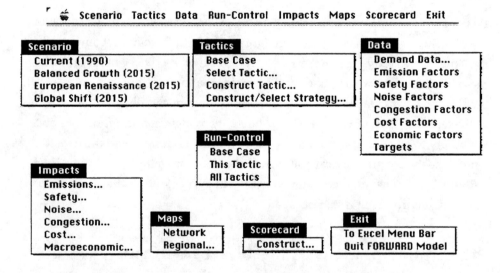

Figure 3.3—PACE-FORWARD's Menu of Capabilities

From Excel, PACE-FORWARD inherits a spreadsheet environment and a GUI to which can be added custom menus and buttons (objects) that trigger actions. Some of these items let the user navigate through the DSS, and others let him or her evaluate tactics by computing and displaying impact measures. Although little effort was devoted to the design and implementation of the GUI, it proved adequate for the needs of various study analysts in both the United States and the Netherlands. It would have to be enhanced, however, if the DSS were to serve users in, say, the Ministry, because the informal DSS support network used as part of the FORWARD study would not be available.

It is through the GUI that PACE-FORWARD conveys to the analyst the policy analysis conceptual framework. The terms *scenario, policy, strategy, measure of performance, cost benefit*, etc., are part of the lexicon of policy analysis. These are used on the various menus, dialogs, and other displays of PACE-FORWARD's GUI. Furthermore, the menus are designed to help the user maintain a top-level view of the analysis problem. At the same time, they provide a means for navigating through the analysis process, from specifying a scenario and tactic to assessing the tactic and examining its measures of performance or impacts. (In the menu bar at the top of Figure 3.3, the first five menu groups shown from left to right represent a typical sequence of analysis steps.)

Tactic Assessment and What-If Capabilities

Having selected an entry from the Scenario menu (see Figure 3.3), an analyst uses the Tactics menu to select a tactic for assessment, at which point a dialog box like the one in Figure 3.4 appears. The dialog box in the display serves as a way to categorize the tactics into shorter, more manageable lists for the user. Its buttons show some of the primitive functions for adding, deleting, and, in general, maintaining tactics in its database. After selecting a tactic, pressing the OK button lets the user verify a subset of the parameters associated with that tactic (see Figure 3.5) and gives an idea of how the tactic is represented in the DSS. In this case, the use of low sulfur fuel for the tactic (build cleaner engines) is implemented via a multiplicative factor of 0.2 to account for an 80 percent reduction in sulfur dioxide (SO_2) emissions. The more complicated parts of representing lower emissions resulting from this tactic are represented in a model/file identified by the name emisfac2, as displayed in Figure 3.5.

After verifying the values on this display, the analyst may execute the tactic assessment via models (by pressing the "This Tactic" button on the control panel—see Figure 3.2) and then display the various impact measures (by selecting, e.g., Emissions on the menu of capabilities—see Figure 3.3).

The GUI also provides a menu that triggers an assessment of all the tactics in the database, summarizing the resulting impact measures on a scorecard that can be used outside the DSS for subsequent ranking of the tactics (see Hillestad et al., 1996).

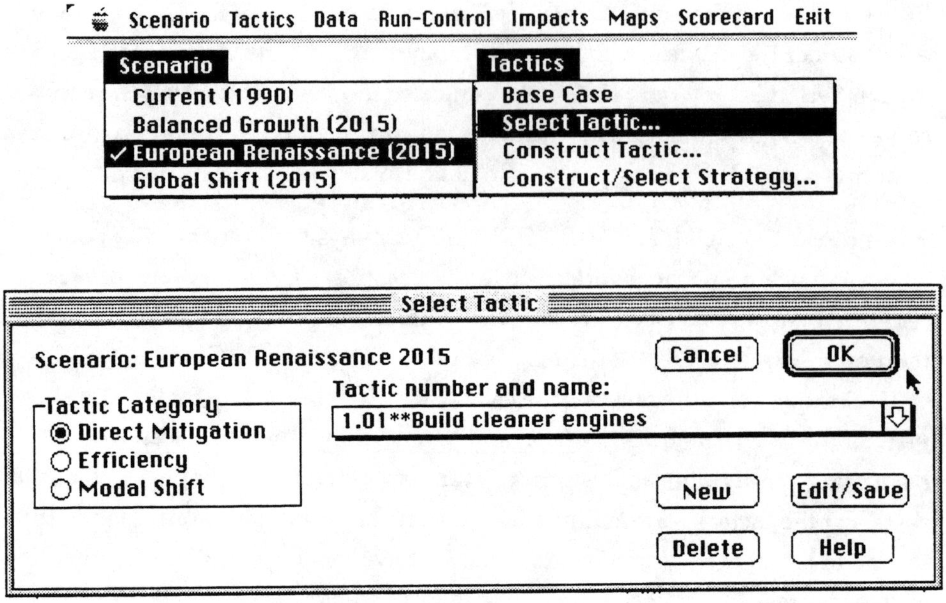

12

Figure 3.4—User Choices in Selecting a Tactic

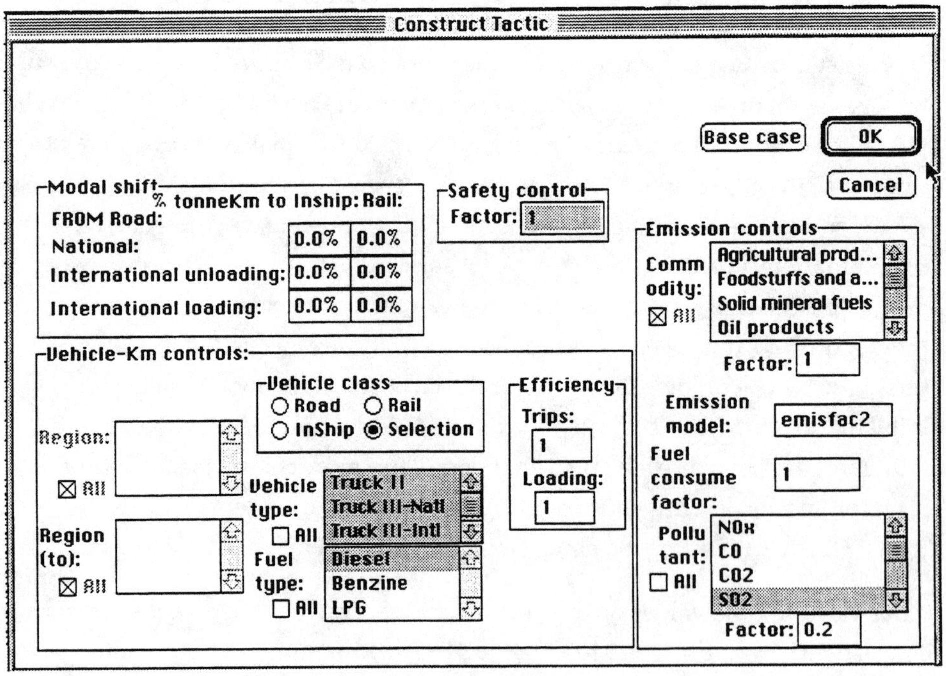

Figure 3.5—Display for Verifying a Tactic

The various factors and mode shift percentages shown in Figure 3.5 add a useful what-if capability to PACE-FORWARD: changing these factors allows the analyst to investigate variations of a tactic or to get bounds on the maximum or minimum payoff of a tactic.

An Example of the Data Analysis Capability

The database management system capabilities of Excel version 4 are rather basic (version 5 [Microsoft Corporation, 1994] has made improvements). Therefore, an expanded query capability had to be developed and added to the PACE-FORWARD DSS for data analysis. Figures 3.6 and 3.7 give an overview of that capability.

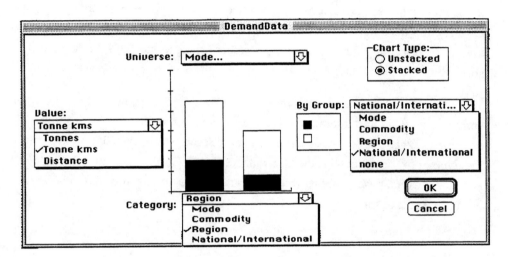

Figure 3.6—User Choices in Selecting the Type of Data Analysis

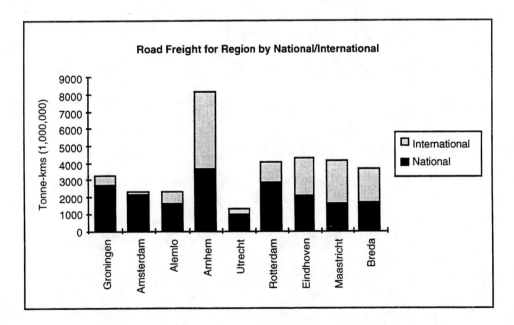

Figure 3.7—Sample Bar Chart Generated by Data Analysis

Figure 3.6 shows the dialog box through which the user requests a query of origin-destination freight estimates from the database of transport flows. This dialog requires prior selection of a scenario through the control panel menus (see Figure 3.3). Then, by clicking a radio button to select a chart type and highlighting an entry from each drop-down list (by first clicking on the downward-pointing arrow), the user specifies what data summary is to be graphed. The user then clicks the OK button of the dialog. The database management system extensions programmed into the DSS respond by constructing the database query to select the appropriate records in the database and then performing the aggregations necessary to generate a graph. Figure 3.7 shows an example of the bar charts that can be generated.

This example of the data analysis process also describes how the DSS components work and interact with one another (refer to Figure 3.1). It shows how the DSS control programs have to display some part of the GUI (in this case, the dialog box), interact with the DSS database management system (which accesses the data base, processes a query), and display the results in another part of the GUI (the graph).

4. The Data, the Models, and Their Integration

As discussed in Section 1, we are using the term *database* to refer to a closely related set of data usually stored under a common entity, such as a table or a file—for example, PACE-FORWARD has a database of freight flows and a database of emission factors. The collection of all PACE-FORWARD databases is referred to as the *data base,* and, by analogy, the collection of models is called the *model base.*

The Data Base

The PACE-FORWARD data base was built mainly from data extracted from external, original data sources (see Figure 3.1). Here, we give an overview of the major databases constructed from the original sources and of the data aggregation required. The major PACE-FORWARD databases are

- Current and projected freight transport flows.
- Aggregate transport networks.
- Vehicle specifications that enter as impact model parameters.
- Vehicle usage data.
- Base-case results for all impacts to serve as a yardstick of comparison for tactic assessment.
- List of tactics and parameters associated with tactic representation for the impact models.

The database of base-case results is a collection of the PACE-FORWARD impacts produced by running the models without selecting a tactic. Therefore, this database is not associated with an external database.

Freight Transport Flows

This database of origin-destination flows has actual freight transport data for 1986 and projections for the year 2015 for three different economic scenarios. The original data were obtained from NEA (1993a). Details on the original data and the data used by PACE-FORWARD are given in Table 4.1.

The commodity classes originally identified by a two-digit NSTR code were aggregated up to the one-digit NSTR level.[1] (The NSTR categorization was apparently designed to allow this type of aggregation.) The fifty-four Dutch traffic regions used in the original data (related to the Transport Economic Model [TEM]) were grouped into the nine Dutch TASC zones, following the example of a previous study (NEA, 1992b). Traffic regions in other countries were grouped into four regions in Germany, two in Belgium, and one for the rest of the world. This was consistent with the fact that Germany and Belgium account for the bulk of the Netherlands international freight transport flows in the transport modes studied. The various flow types in the original NEA data were aggregated down to a single type.

The aggregate freight flow data (described here) and the shortest distances between pairs of network nodes (described below) were combined to obtain a tonne and tonne-kilometer database of freight flows. Accessed through the Data menu, this database is used by PACE-FORWARD for explorations of transport flows.

A still more aggregated database derived from the tonne and tonne-kilometer database was constructed for the traffic conversion model for use in computing vehicle-kilometers. This database has tables of tonne-kilometers for each of the ten commodity classes and nine Dutch TASC geographic zones. For each mode of transport, three tables are kept: national, international unloaded in the

Table 4.1

Aggregation of Freight Transport Flows

Attributes	Original Data Source	PACE-FORWARD
Economic scenarios[a]	4	4
Modes of transport[b]	3	3
NSTR commodity classes	53	10
Geographic regions	54/72	9(14 nodes)/7
(network nodes)	Dutch/foreign	Dutch/foreign
Flow types	9	1

SOURCE: NEA, 1993a.

[a]The four scenarios consist of one "current" year scenario and three scenarios for the year 2015: balanced growth, European renaissance, and global shift.

[b]The three modes are road, inland waterway, and rail.

---

[1]NSTR = *Nomenclature uniforme des marchandises pour les Statistiques de Transport, Revisée.*

Netherlands, and international loaded in the Netherlands.[2] This database of transport flows is used by the emission impact models, among others.

Transport Networks for Road, Rail, and Inland Waterway

Networks were constructed to include the major freight routes for the three modes of transport considered by the FORWARD study—road, rail, and inland waterway. These networks include fourteen origin-destination nodes in the Netherlands, two in Belgium, and four in Germany; they include all major freight transport centers in the Netherlands. For the various links of these networks, distance data were gathered from many sources, including road, rail, and other geographical maps.

Vehicle Specifications That Enter as Impact Model Parameters

The parameters of the DSS models (e.g., emission factors, characteristics per vehicle) were based on many sources (discussed later, in Sections 5 through 10). These parameters are associated with the base case for each scenario.

Vehicle capacity and utilization factors were taken from a previous study (Blok et al., 1992, Appendix 3),[3] as were the vehicle type categorizations used:

- Van: 1.0–1.5 tonnes (in three fuel subcategories[4])

- Truck type I: 1.5–10 tonnes

- Truck type II: 10–18 tonnes

- Truck type III: >18 tonnes

- Ship type I: 21–650 tonnes

- Ship type II: 650–1500 tonnes

- Ship type III: >1500 tonnes

- Trains

PACE-FORWARD assumes that all trucks use diesel fuel.

---

[2]For one transport mode, inland waterway, the national tonne-kilometer table is actually broken down further into two demand categories, tanker and nontanker.

[3]These data were carried in the database in at least the same level of detail as they had been carried in the original source—e.g., commercial versus a company's own transport (for national transport for road and inland waterway), tanker versus nontanker (for inland waterway).

[4]As an extension to the Blok study, we considered three fuel types: gasoline, diesel, and liquefied petroleum gas (LPG).

Vehicle Usage Data

Most of the data on vehicle usage came from Blok et al. (1992, Appendix 3). They include average annual distance traveled, average distance per trip, average vehicle load, and maximum capacity for the various vehicle types and the three modes of transport. Because of the volume of data involved, they are not shown here.

Tactics

The Ministry, stakeholders, and RAND/EAC personnel all took part in putting together the list of freight transport tactics. Researching the tactics with a view to incorporating them into the DSS was the job of a RAND/EAC multidisciplinary team. Estimates of model parameters associated with each tactic were either obtained from the numerous sources available or were based on work discussed in the relevant literature (see Appendix C of Hillestad et al., 1996).

How best to represent a tactic in the DSS model and data base was mainly left to the DSS developer. This process was slow at first, because the models were still under development. Later in the study, however, as more experience was gained and the capabilities and weaknesses of the models became apparent, the process sped up substantially.

Data Extraction Process

The data extraction process involved in building the DSS data base included data aggregation and conversion. A representative example of data aggregation is described above, within the discussion of freight transport flows.

Carrying the level of detail of the original data files into the DSS in all cases would have resulted in a cumbersome and unmanageable data base. A decision was thus made early in the DSS design and development to aggregate the geographic regions, the commodity classes, and the so-called flow types. This decision was based on a preliminary analysis of the data. Thus, for example, our data aggregation scheme not only results in a leaner database, but also retains the separation of important regions (nationally and internationally), such as Rotterdam, and of important commodity classes, such as the one that groups foodstuffs, animal fodder, and agricultural products.

Our data conversion efforts ranged from the simple to the advanced. One of the simple conversions entailed scaling up transport flows to obtain 1990 freight flow estimates from 1986 data. One of the advanced conversions involved the use of a shortest-path algorithm to obtain the shortest path and distance between any origin-destination pair in a road network. For each set of path and distance, the resulting tonne-kilometers can be prorated to the links of that path. Floyd's shortest-path algorithm (see Hu, 1969, for example) was used; an implementation was built using spreadsheets and C language code in the form of Macintosh code resources.[5]

The Model Base

The DSS model base for freight transport includes models for

- Mode shift based on cost elasticities
- Traffic conversion (from tonne-kms to vehicle-kms)
- Air-pollutant emissions
- Safety
- Noise
- Congestion
- Cost
- Macroeconomic effects

For the data and models to be integrated within the PACE-FORWARD DSS, each model must receive inputs that either are in the data base or are intermediate outputs of the other models. Some of the steps taken to achieve model integration included using consistent data, achieving model consistency by having the traffic conversion model be the common driver of all the other models, and enhancing the models so that they could accept data at the appropriate level of aggregation. Achieving data and model consistency simplified the job of integration.

The methodology used in the PACE-FORWARD DSS models was derived mainly from existing models. However, when a new model had to be designed or an existing model had to be enhanced, we made sure that the resulting model had the appropriate level of resolution and that its required data could be obtained within the analysis time frame of the FORWARD study.

These modeling issues are discussed in more detail in the following paragraphs.

---

[5]The ability to run compiled-language code resources (called dynamic link libraries in the IBM PC environment) was an Excel feature that led to the use of the Excel environment in developing PACE-FORWARD.

Data Consistency

An example should clarify this issue. There are different types of vehicle-kilometer estimating methodologies. The approach used by the Netherlands Economic Institute (NEI) is based on tonnage-flow estimates as well as vehicle capacities and fill rates. Another approach, one used in some estimates from the Dutch Central Bureau of Statistics (CBS), apparently relies on counts of vehicle registrations and estimates of average annual distances traveled by vehicles. For consistency in PACE-FORWARD, we used the NEI methodology and data consistent with it.

Traffic Conversion Model

The traffic conversion model, which estimates vehicle-kilometers, is based on existing methodology (Blok et al., 1992, pp. 9–10). This model computes vehicle-kilometers by dividing transport flows (in tonne-kilometers) by an adjusted vehicle load (in tonnes) that takes into consideration the average fill rate when a vehicle is loaded with cargo and the percentage of the total distance traveled during which it is loaded (i.e., not empty).[6] The derivation of tonne-kilometers thus uses projected freight transport flows; transport networks for roads, rail, and inland waterways; and vehicle specifications and usage data—all of which are described above.

The traffic conversion model derives the number of vehicle-kilometers by a number of attributes:

- Mode: road, inland waterway, and rail.

- Vehicle type (see discussion of vehicle specifications, above): for road, three van types and three truck types for national transport, and one truck type for international transport; for inland waterway, three ship types, further categorized for national transport into tanker and nontanker carriers; for rail, one vehicle type.

- Ten (one-digit NSTR) commodity classes.

- Nine Dutch aggregate geographical (TASC) zones.

---

[6]This approach differs from that used by CBS, which, as stated above, appears to be based on vehicle registrations and estimates of average distance traveled per vehicle per year. Substantial discrepancies between the results of these two approaches warrant resolution in a subsequent effort (given that both approaches have been used in previous studies sponsored by the Dutch government).

These data are passed, directly or indirectly, to all impact models and are the main drivers of the results. They are therefore major contributors to the consistency of the impact models.

Model Enhancement and Data Aggregation

To achieve consistency, different types of adaptations were carried out on the models and data. We give a sampling of those adaptations here.

The original NEI traffic conversion model could not handle the added attributes of three van types and the categorizations by ten commodity types and nine geographical regions. We generalized the NEI model to deal with these new attributes and categories.

NEI's vehicle utilization rates and capacities were available for a specific set of vehicle categories. For example, international freight transport leaving the Netherlands was differentiated from that arriving in the Netherlands. When the NEA freight flow data were aggregated, that differentiation was maintained so that we could fully utilize the NEI vehicle capacity data.

Another adaptation concerns the TNO (Netherlands Organization for Applied Scientific Research) air-pollutant emission models for trucks. Since the NEI truck data carried detail on various transport categories (including truck types, whether the transport was national or international, private or commercial, etc.), the TNO model was generalized so that it could handle all of these data categories and then lead to suitable aggregations across the transport categories.

In the end, the output from the traffic conversion model (vehicle-kilometers across many categories) is aggregated to the level of resolution required by the various impact models. Again, the end result is consistency that has been achieved by using the same source.

Integration

As already noted, existing models had to be extended and data had to be aggregated in order to achieve the consistency required for integration. If nonproprietary (thus accessible) model implementations had been used, they would have required major reprogramming of models that were written in different computer languages, operating in different computer environments, or insufficiently documented as to implementation details. The envisioned difficulties of a major reprogramming effort effectively ruled out the use of existing model implementations.

An environment in which to integrate models requires a variety of capabilities to support (at least) the database and model base management systems. If tools for user interaction are required—as is the case for policy analysis—then something such as a GUI is needed. A quick search for existing software products with the capabilities we sought led us to the Excel spreadsheet environment.

Level of Resolution

Every model is a representation of "reality" at some level of detail, the choice of level depending on what types of questions one expects to answer in using the model. For our case, in which the objective was a policy analysis of freight transport tactics, the resolution level of the DSS models had to be sufficient for capturing the costs and benefits of every tactic studied. During the FORWARD study, decisions concerning the models' level of resolution dealt with a moving target: the more difficult tactics, which were added last to the DSS, usually required new capabilities. Thus, the initial models in the DSS had to evolve over time into more sophisticated approaches as they needed to handle more difficult tactics.[7]

Related to decisions on the level of model resolution were decisions on the level of data aggregation to be used in building the DSS data base. Decisions on the level of aggregation had to be made early in the FORWARD study, especially given the limited database capabilities of Excel version 4. However, the chosen level could then constrain the ability to accurately represent tactics entered into the DSS data base at a later time.

For example, the aggregation (done outside the DSS) of original freight flow data into tonne-kilometers by Dutch zone and transport mode collapses the network link detail. These aggregated data are used by most of the impact models in the DSS.[8] A problem arises, however, if a later tactic involves changing the freight flow between two nodes (e.g., major transport centers) of a network, in which case a way has to be found to represent this change in the models without having to rerun the regional aggregation outside the DSS.

---

[7]One requirement of a DSS is that it allow for evolution or change of the problem, data, and methodology. The PACE-FORWARD DSS design and implementation did successfully grow and evolve over the duration of the study. Even though the embedded models were enhanced numerous times, the GUI remained rather stable throughout the study. Credit for a smooth evolution goes to an effective configuration control.

[8]The data analysis tools of PACE-FORWARD can still obtain freight flows (tonnes and tonne-kilometers) between any origin-destination pair of Dutch and foreign zones, but only for each scenario's base case.

For a policy analysis of tactics affecting freight transport, there is no way to achieve a level of resolution that meets all needs, because one can always construct a tactic that requires greater modeling detail than what is currently provided. The existing level of modeling resolution was based on the types of answers expected from the DSS, the structure of the problem, the available data, the time, the budget, and other resources available to the analysis.[9] The PACE-FORWARD DSS proved to be suitable for the circumstances of the FORWARD study.

The Model Base Management System

The DSS model base management system orchestrates the interface between the models and databases and the interconnection by which models pass their intermediate results. For some tactics, it was more efficient to create new models than to carry numerous parameters. It was then the job of the model base management system to select and execute the appropriate model.

Model Creation

Adding new tactics to the database of tactics was an important part of constructing the PACE-FORWARD DSS. The emission models alone required over one hundred parameters. Instead of carrying this many emission parameters (in addition to the parameters of the other models) for each tactic in the data base, it was more efficient to have several emission models and to have the database of tactics specify which air-pollutant emission model to use with each tactic.

When a tactic requires a new emission model, one is created with the base-case emission model as the default. The model, represented in spreadsheets, can then be tailored to the needs of that tactic's representation, by changing either the model parameter values or the formulas used.

Currently, there are only a few user-friendly tools in the DSS that a typical user could use to add new tactics and to add and point to the appropriate air-pollutant emission model. Since the task of tailoring emission models to tactics many times requires in-depth knowledge of the emission model methodology, we concluded that the actual addition of new emission models is a job better suited for the DSS advanced user or model developer.

---

[9]For example, time and budgetary constraints were a factor in the decision not to aggregate data by regions for the noise model, which uses data for seventy-four individual road links instead.

Interface with Data Base

The models access the DSS data base through hard-coded (formula) links kept in the spreadsheet models or through dynamic links established at execution time by the Excel control programs of the DSS.

5. Costing of Tactics

The Cost Model

Because PACE-FORWARD is designed to evaluate proposed transport tactics, it is mainly interested in the changes that a tactic brings about in cost and other measures of performance compared to a base case. An attempt was made to be comprehensive in identifying the costs associated with a tactic, but no attempt was made to capture the transitional costs incurred when a tactic is initially implemented.

The cost model developed was a first attempt to bring costs together from many sources. We had to be pragmatic in using existing data; for example, the cost categories we identified were either already available in existing data or could be added with reasonable effort.

The transport scenarios for a given year in the DSS data base provide estimates of transport flows by mode in terms of tonne-kilometers by ten commodity classes. Our transport cost estimates for these scenarios use costing methodology from previous studies (McKinsey, 1992; Knight-Wendling Consultants BV, 1992), where transport cost is estimated on the basis of tonnes and tonne-kilometers by mode, with a further breakdown based on whether the freight can be considered bulk. The transport cost rates used can be derived from the data given in Tables 5.1 and 5.2.

Table 5.1

Estimates of Freight Transport Costs, by Mode

Cost[a] Type	Freight Type	Road	Inland Waterway	Rail	Units
Fixed[b]	Bulk	22	15	27	Dfl[c]/tonne
	Other	20	41	48	Dfl/tonne
Variable	Bulk	0.18	0.01	0.042	Dfl/tonne-km
	Other	0.18	0.027	0.053	Dfl/tonne-km

SOURCE: Knight-Wendling Consultants BV, 1992.
[a]Includes investment and operating costs.
[b]Loading, unloading, and transshipment costs.
[c]Dutch florins.

Table 5.2

Estimates of Bulk Percentage, by Commodity Class

NSTR Commodity Class		Bulk (%)	Other (%)
0	Agricultural products and live animals	70	30
1	Foodstuffs and animal fodder	35	65
2	Solid mineral fuels	100	0
3	Oil products	100	0
4	Ores and metal waste	100	0
5	Metal products	0	100
6	Crude and manufactured minerals, building materials	60	40
7	Fertilizers	100	0
8	Chemicals	70	30
9	Other goods and products	0	100

SOURCE: RAND/EAC estimates.

To compute time costs, the PACE-FORWARD cost model relies on Ministry-sponsored work by the Dutch firm NEI (see Bozuwa, 1994b, for data and methodology). NEI provided estimates of costs per tonne-hour of transport delay (see Table 5.3).

For infrastructure investment costs by mode, existing cost estimates for a tactic were used when available; otherwise, estimates were made based on previous studies of similar tactics or estimates in other literature sources. Infrastructure costs were amortized over a period of years consistent with the estimated durability of the infrastructure and the magnitude of the estimated infrastructure costs (one, ten, or fifty years).

Table 5.3

Estimates of Time Costs, by Commodity Class
(Dfl/tonne-hour)

NSTR Commodity Class		Road	Inland Waterway	Rail
0	Agricultural products and live animals	3.06	0.43	1.01
1	Foodstuffs and animal fodder	4.23	0.60	1.39
2	Solid mineral fuels	0.49	0.07	0.16
3	Oil products	1.50	0.21	0.50
4	Ores and metal waste	0.83	0.12	0.27
5	Metal products	2.80	0.40	0.92
6	Crude and manufactured minerals, building materials	0.18	0.03	0.06
7	Fertilizers	1.23	0.17	0.40
8	Chemicals	2.40	0.34	0.79
9	Other goods and products	13.63	1.93	4.49

SOURCE: Bozuwa, 1994b.

Cost Categories

Cost categories are normally selected on the basis of how the costs are to be used.[1] Thus, one could consider categorizations that separate investment from operating costs, fixed costs from variable costs, or private company costs from public, government costs. Still another possibility is a categorization that separates true costs from the return on investment expected by companies in the transport business.

For the FORWARD study, tactic screening only required total net cost change from the base case for the scenario used. However, PACE-FORWARD's use of nonoverlapping cost categories, a choice based on the ease of model implementation, proved very helpful in verifying and validating the models. Across tactics, the comparison of costs in the various categories was also helpful in screening the tactics.

Most of the cost categories we used dealt with variable costs that could readily be computed from cost factors and transport variables internal to the traffic conversion model and other PACE-FORWARD impact models. These costs apply to either the base case or the tactics. They include costs that can be computed as a function of the following (see Figure 5.1):

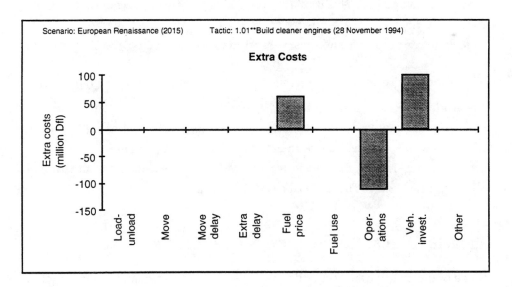

Figure 5.1—Resulting Cost Breakdown for a Tactic

---

[1]In general, cost changes can be assumed to be passed to the "consumers" as changes in prices or tariffs. Therefore, although the term *cost* is used throughout this section, in many cases the term *price* could have been used instead.

- Tonnes transported per transport mode and commodity class, which makes costs sensitive to mode shift or a change in scenario (labeled "Load-unload" in Figure 5.1). The costs per tonne used are shown in Table 5.1.

- Tonne-kilometers transported per mode, which makes costs sensitive to mode shift or a change in scenario (labeled "Move"). The costs per tonne-kilometer used are shown in Table 5.1.

- Kilometers traveled per mode, which makes costs sensitive to changes in fuel price or in fuel consumption per distance traveled (labeled "Fuel price" and "Fuel use," respectively). The per-unit cost of fuel was obtained from CBS, 1992a.

- Hours of travel, making costs sensitive to the time it takes for a mode shift (labeled "Move delay"). Estimates of the time costs used are shown in Table 5.3.

- Number of vehicles in the fleet, making costs sensitive to changes in life-cycle annualized vehicle replacement costs or annual maintenance costs (labeled "Veh. invest." and "Operations," respectively). Per-vehicle cost changes in these categories were estimated for the tactics.

A few other of the cost categories used dealt with fixed or variable costs that were entered into PACE-FORWARD accounting mostly as parameters because they could not readily be estimated from its models and parameters. These were specific to certain tactics and thus were estimated outside the DSS. They include

- Infrastructure annualized investment costs (labeled "Other" in Figure 5.1).

- Additional travel distance and time necessitated by mode shift and not otherwise captured. For example, a mode shift to rail requires driving an extra distance to the train terminal and then unloading and loading again. Also, there is the estimated additional time/distance from the train terminal to the customer. (These are labeled "Extra delay.")

Effects of Cost Changes on Modal Shift

Some of the freight transport tactics being assessed expected a certain amount of mode shift, say, from road to inland waterway. A difficulty arises in estimating what amount of mode shift will be achieved by tactics whose incentives involve cost or pricing changes.

In PACE-FORWARD, the analyst can deal with this problem in one of two ways. He or she can bound the tactic's payoff by assuming a maximal mode shift for the freight volume considered, such as mode shifting to rail all the road freight currently leaving Rotterdam for Germany. For these cases of maximal mode shift, conservation of tonne-kilometers is assumed, because implementation details (e.g., the pricing steps that achieve the maximal mode shift) are being ignored: the tonne-kilometers just shift from one mode to another. This approach may be sufficient for estimating the order of magnitude of the payoff.

The second approach, which is used by some transport tactics in PACE-FORWARD, takes pricing information into consideration. A model estimates the modal shift from any one of the three transport modes (road, rail, inland waterway) to another based on estimated price elasticities. This modal shift model is based on previous research by Blok (1993b, pp. 35–36) and Oum (1989). Inputs are the percent changes in transport prices. As with any elasticity model, only relatively small deviations with respect to the current transport system should be used. Major changes, especially over the long run, are likely to trigger any number of unpredictable adaptations in the system and therefore are not amenable to modeling.

The Cost Model in Perspective

The cost model implemented in PACE-FORWARD tries to capture tactic-related changes in total transport costs to the transport system stakeholders. Changes in costs in the various categories shown in Figure 5.1 can help identify which stakeholders are affected. For example, a tax on fuel could increase transporters' operations costs (which may be passed to consumers) as well as government revenues. In this case, Figure 5.1 would explicitly show the effects on transporters but not the effect on the government or consumers.

As another example, the government could require the use of new engines that, when compared with those in current use, are more expensive to buy and operate but less polluting. The corresponding Figure 5.1 would explicitly show the transporters' increased vehicle investment and operations costs but, again, not the effect on consumers.

To further track the effect of tactics across the sectors of the economy—and thus to identify shifts across sectors—PACE-FORWARD includes a macroeconomic impact model (see Section 10).

As mentioned earlier, the political and implementation issues related to the tactics were excluded from the FORWARD study and therefore from the DSS as well. This means that any subsequent study covering such issues needs to pay more attention (than was possible in FORWARD) to who is affected by the costs or benefits associated with a tactic. It may be that a tactic does not change the total costs but does shift costs from the transport sector to the government, or from one part of the transport sector to another. Clearly, these effects raise issues that need to be addressed outside the DSS because of their political implications.

6. The Models for Emissions

Models

The models used in PACE-FORWARD for air-pollutant emissions are based on work performed by NEI (Blok et al., 1992, p. 10) and TNO (Klein, 1993). These models generate estimates of emissions of hydrocarbons (C_mH_n), oxides of nitrogen (NO_x), carbon dioxide (CO_2), carbon monoxide (CO), particulates/ aerosols, and sulfur dioxide (SO_2). Figures 6.1 and 6.2 show typical DSS emission displays.[1]

For all vehicle types except trucks, the air-pollutant emissions are proportional to the number of vehicle-kilometers, where the factors of proportionality are constant emission rates. This approach, covering vans, inland waterway ships, and trains, is consistent with NEI's previous work (Blok et al., 1992, p. 10).

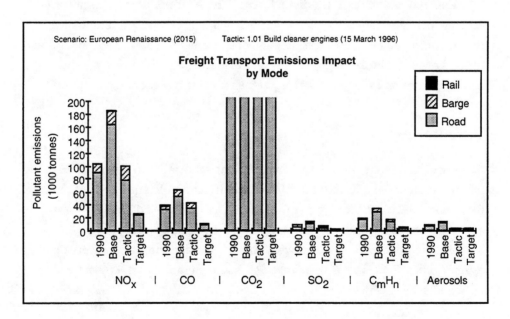

Figure 6.1—Air-Pollutant Emissions Due to Freight Transport

---

[1]Figure 6.1 focuses on the majority of the pollutants, resulting in a truncation of the values for CO_2 (the user may change the vertical scale to show the full CO_2 detail). The legend entries of Figure 6.2 can be further explained by way of an example: "% road fr. only/all freight" should be interpreted as percent road freight emissions relative to all freight emissions.

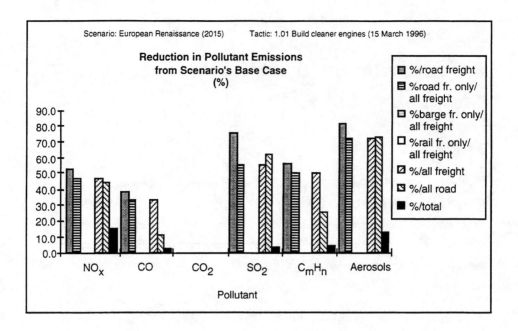

Figure 6.2—Total Air-Pollutant Emissions for a Tactic

The TNO models are used for diesel trucks. These air-pollutant emission models assume that emissions are directly proportional to fuel consumption, which in turn is computed as a nonlinear function of a number of parameters, including truck capacity, vehicle weight (empty and loaded), air resistance, etc. This truck fuel consumption model is described at the end of this section.

Parameters

Base-case parameters for the truck emission models are given below. Truck parameters that have to do with vehicle capacity and utilization were taken from Blok et al., 1992, Appendix 3. For the other vehicles modeled, the base-case emission rates are as given in Tables 6.1 and 6.2. Parameters for the emission models that are tactic dependent were obtained from technical literature or estimated based on similar work reported in the literature (see Appendix C of Hillestad et al., 1996).

Fuel Consumption Model for Trucks

The discussion in this concluding subsection is technical and is provided for completeness.

Table 6.1

Air-Pollutant Emission Rates for Vans
(grams/vehicle-kilometers)

Pollutant		Diesel	Gasoline	LPG
C_mH_n	Hydrocarbons	0.46	3.3	1.8
NO_x	Oxides of nitrogen	1.10	3.00	2.30
CO_2	Carbon dioxide	280.00	253.00	206.00
CO	Carbon monoxide	1.4	19	4.2
	Aerosols	0.31	0.056	0.023
SO_2	Sulfur dioxide	0.29	0.036	0

SOURCE: CBS, 1992b, p. 48.

Table 6.2

Air-Pollutant Emission Rates for Trains and Inland Waterway Ships
(grams/vehicle-kilometers)

Pollutant		Trains	Inland Waterway Ships	
			National	International
C_mH_n	Hydrocarbons	0.4	18.8	30.5
NO_x	Oxides of nitrogen	26.9	106.2	172.2
CO_2	Carbon dioxide[a]	8336	7698.6	7698.6
			16040.4	16040.4
			33527.4	33527.4
CO	- Carbon monoxide	1.4	45.3	73.5
	Aerosols	0.8	7.7	12.4
SO_2	Sulfur dioxide	21.5	14.5	23.5

SOURCE: Blok et al., 1992, pp. 10–11.

[a]The three emission rates shown for ships correspond to the three ship types:
I (21-650 tonnes), II (650-1500 tonnes), and III (>1500 tonnes).

Under the TNO method (Klein, 1993), truck air-pollutant emissions are directly proportional to fuel consumption:[2]

$$\text{emissions (g/vehicle-km)} = \sum C^i \, b_v{}^i \, P^i / 1000$$

where the summation is over the trip types i (see Table 6.3), b_v is fuel consumption (in grams of fuel per kilometer), C is emission rate for a given pollutant (in grams of emissions per kilogram of fuel—see Table 6.3), and P^i is the incidence probability for trip type i.

---

[2]This formula applies when emission rates are given in terms of grams per kilogram of fuel units; a similar formula applies when the rates are in grams per liter of fuel.

Table 6.3

Air-Pollutant Emission Rates for Trucks
(grams of pollutant/measure of fuel)

Pollutant		Trip Type[a]	Trucks and Semis[b] 3.5-16 tonnes	Trucks and Semis >16 tonnes	Units
C_mH_n	Hydrocarbons	Built up	12	16	g/kg
		Rural	4	8	
		Highway	4	8	
NO_x	Oxides of nitrogen	Built up	55	50	g/kg
		Rural	70	65	
		Highway	70	65	
CO	Carbon monoxide	Built up	28	20	g/kg
		Rural	14	10	
		Highway	14	10	
	Aerosols	Built up	4.3	4.3	g/kg
		Rural	4.3	4.3	
		Highway	4.3	4.3	
SO_2	Sulfur dioxide	All	2.8	2.8	g/liter
CO_2	Carbon dioxide	All	2630	2630	g/liter

SOURCE: Klein, 1993.

[a] All = built up (e.g., cities), rural, and highway.

[b] Semitrailers.

Fuel consumption (in grams/kilometer) is estimated as

$$b_v = b_r m$$
$$+ b_1 A(25/V_v + V_v^2/1000)$$
$$+ b_k(1 - V_v/100)m$$
$$+ b_{kr}(100/V_v - 1)m_b$$
$$+ b_0(m_b + 10)/V_v$$

where

$$m_n = 0.66(m_b - 1.2) = \text{average loading capacity (tonnes)}$$
$$m_v = m_b - m_n = \text{average vehicle weight (tonnes)}$$
$$m = B_{rt}/100 \; B_{gr}/100 \; m_n + m_v = \text{weight on road (tonnes)}$$

and the values and definitions for the rest of the parameters are as given in Tables 6.4 and 6.5.

Implicit in these data is the fact that the TNO model depends on trip and truck types (see Table 6.4) and truck age (see Table 6.5). Separate data had to be obtained for the incidence of the various trip types (van Minnen, 1992) and the year-of-manufacture profile for trucks (CBS, 1990). In the case of parameters dependent on the year of vehicle manufacture, linear interpolations were performed as needed.

Table 6.4

TNO Fuel Consumption Model: Parameters Dependent on Truck Size

Parameter		Trip Type	Trucks 3.5-16 Tonnes	Trucks >16 Tonnes	Semis	Units
A	Average frontal surface	All	8.6	8.6	8.6	m^2
m_b	Gross allowable weight	All	10	22	35	tonnes
B_{rt}	Loaded trips	All	65	65	65	%
B_{gr}	Average tonne utilization factor	All	75	75	75	%
V_v	Speed (varying)	Built up	19	19	19	km/h
		Rural	50	50	50	km/h
		Highway	80	60	80	km/h

SOURCE: Klein, 1993.

Table 6.5

TNO Fuel Consumption Model: Parameters Dependent on Date of Truck Manufacture

Parameter		Built in Year 1981	Built in Year 1990
b_r	Break roll resistance	1.5×3.5	1.5×3.0
b_l	Break air resistance	1.75	1.35
b_k	Kinetic energy vehicle	11.8	10.7
b_{kr}	Kinetic energy of rotating parts	0.32	0.29
b_0	Consumption per time unit	55.5	50.0

SOURCE: Klein, 1993.

Another complication arose in that the truck capacity and utilization factors were available as a function not just of vehicle type, but also of whether the carrier was internal or external to the company (national transport) and whether the carrier was loading or unloading in the Netherlands (international transport). Generalizations of the TNO methodology were derived to deal with these cases.

7. The Model for Safety

Model

The PACE-FORWARD safety model estimates the number of accident-related injuries and fatalities caused by road freight transport (it excludes injuries and fatalities involving only passenger vehicles). The estimate is directly proportional to the number of vehicle-kilometers, where the factor of proportionality for fatalities and injuries varies by vehicle type. A sample result for a tactic is given in Figure 7.1.

Parameters

The effect of changes in vehicle-kilometers is automatically passed by the traffic conversion model to the safety model. To introduce other effects of the tactics, a multiplier was incorporated into the model. This multiplier was estimated based on accident data from the IMPULS database of the Transport Research Centre of the Ministry (Drie, 1994).

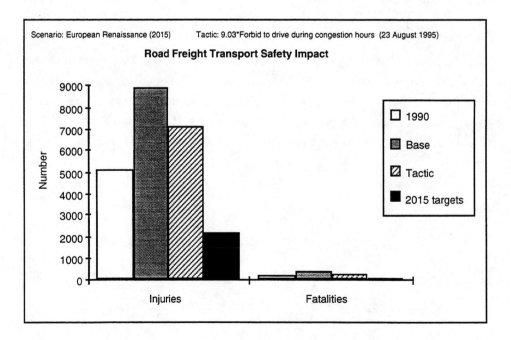

Figure 7.1—Safety Impact Due to Road Freight Traffic

8. The Model for Congestion

Model

The congestion model is new and was derived as part of the FORWARD study. It estimates highway congestion severity—defined as the product of length of congestion and its duration—due to both passenger and freight transport traffic.

For each road link, the model is a nonlinear regression of the ratio of average traffic intensity to road link capacity. The model also has a "last-year" lag term to represent the structural propensity for certain links to have congestion year after year. PACE-FORWARD uses the average across all road links as an aggregate measure of congestion. Figure 8.1 shows a sample display of the congestion measure.

The parameters of the congestion model were obtained using congestion data provided by the Ministry (Bekkers, 1994) for the years 1987 and 1990. When predictions of congestion were made for the year 1991, the results provided a good fit to the actual data for 1991 (data also from the Ministry). The model's mathematical details are given at the end of this section.

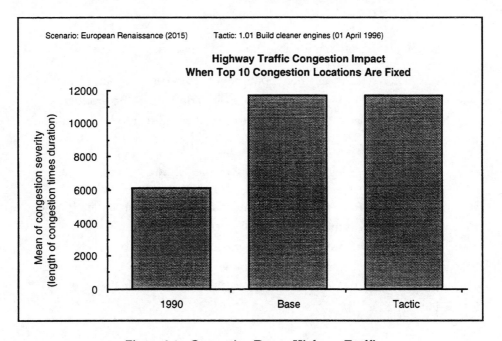

Figure 8.1—Congestion Due to Highway Traffic

It is difficult to predict the extent and locations of congestion in the year 2015, given that current bottlenecks may lead to structural changes (such as the widening of bridges or the construction of new roads) to alleviate a current problem. In estimating congestion for the year 2015, the PACE-FORWARD congestion model assumes that the current distribution of traffic (in time and location) across the road network remains the same unless changed by the tactic being analyzed. However, it allows for the possibility that the worst N number of congestion links in a road network could be enhanced so that they would no longer be among the top N bottlenecks. PACE-FORWARD does this by assuming that the top N = 10 bottlenecks will be alleviated. This assumption changes the magnitude of the congestion measure but not the ordering of tactics according to the noise measure.

Parameters

The traffic conversion model makes a tactic's changes in vehicle-kilometers available to the congestion model, which uses them to compute a multiplicative factor consisting of the change in traffic intensity with respect to the 1990 base case. This and a second multiplicative factor are then used as inputs for that tactic to the congestion model. The second multiplicative factor, which provides a means for incorporating congestion effects not related to vehicle-kilometers, is estimated outside the DSS and kept in the database of tactics.

Methodology

The technical discussion in this subsection is provided for completeness.

The PACE-FORWARD congestion model covers both passenger and freight transport traffic. Let G be the congestion severity defined as the product of length of congestion and its duration. Then, the congestion model used is the following regression:

$$\log G = \alpha + \beta * [ki / c] + \log G_b + \varepsilon$$

where α and β are parameters to be estimated from the historical data for the road network links, k is the intensity-multiplier parameter associated with a tactic, i/c is the ratio of intensity to capacity, G_b is the congestion severity for a base year, and ε is an error term. The parameters α and β are estimated with 1987 and 1990 data (1990 is the base year) with $k = 1$. This was done outside PACE-FORWARD.

A random error was generated for 1000 replications, and regressed values of the congestion severity G were obtained for each link of the road network and for intensity multipliers k ranging from 0.7 to 2.0. This simulation allowed computation of the mean, the standard deviation, and other statistics that capture the uncertainty of the estimates. However, PACE-FORWARD only uses the means averaged across all the links in the road network.

This average congestion severity for k ranging from 0.7 to 2.0 provided a table of results (Table 8.1) that can be looked up in PACE-FORWARD and interpolated with the actual estimate of k for a tactic. Also shown in Table 8.1 is the average congestion severity when five, ten, and twenty of the most congested links are assumed fixed (and thus are no longer among the top bottlenecks). These serve to mimic situations in which future construction removes structural congestion problems.

Table 8.1

Average Congestion Severity as a Function of Traffic Intensity
(length of congestion × duration)

Intensity Multiplier k	Links Fixed			
	0	5	10	20
0.7	3844	3623	3514	3389
0.8	4613	4331	4196	4043
0.9	5557	5195	5028	4841
1.0	6718	6253	6046	5816
1.1	8151	7552	7294	7012
1.2	9927	9153	8830	8483
1.3	12136	11132	10728	10299
1.4	14891	13585	13079	12548
1.5	18340	16637	16001	15343
1.6	22675	20446	19646	18828
1.7	28142	25217	24209	23187
1.8	35060	31210	29937	28660
1.9	43848	38766	37156	35554
2.0	55050	48323	46282	44268

SOURCE: RAND.

9. The Model for Noise

Model

The PACE-FORWARD model for highway noise is taken from Article 102 of the Dutch noise nuisance law (Ministry of Housing, Physical Planning, and Environment, 1981), modified slightly, as noted below.

The model, which is quite detailed, represents noise emissions based on vehicle characteristics and traffic data. For example, it tracks three vehicle types—light (including passenger vehicles), medium (light trucks), and heavy—either during the day or night.[1]

Although this model estimates the noise for each road link examined,[2] an overall aggregate measure of noise impact is also computed, for the purpose of tactic comparison. PACE-FORWARD uses an aggregate measure of noise performance that is the weighted average distance from the highway at which the noise level for each link falls below 55 dB(A);[3] the weights in this average are the fraction of length of each link over the total length of the links in the network. A sample display of this noise measure in shown in Figure 9.1.

Parameters

PACE-FORWARD assumes that the current distribution of traffic in time and location is maintained in 2015 unless explicitly changed by a tactic.

Changes for a tactic in any of the vehicle-kilometer categories computed by the DSS traffic conversion model are always available to the noise model. To generalize the Dutch noise model, we revised it to accept tactic-specific factors that either were estimated or were derived from the vehicle-kilometers. The following tactic-specific factors depend on vehicle type:

---

[1] The model could also represent the noise of motorcycles; however, data were not readily available for them.

[2] PACE-FORWARD uses the noise model with traffic intensity data for seventy-four links of a road network, as provided by the Ministry (Bekkers, 1994).

[3] In the noise and other environmental impact models, we did not use measures of performance that estimate the number of people affected. These alternative measures would have required population density data not readily available to the FORWARD study.

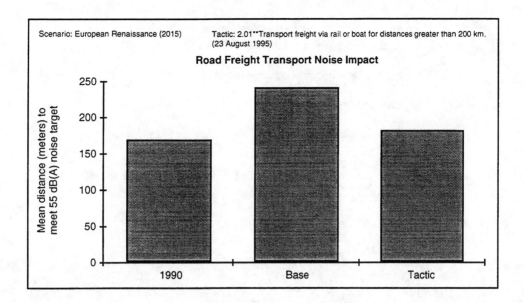

Figure 9.1—Noise Due to Highway Traffic

- The traffic intensity factor, which is based on a change in estimated vehicle-kilometers.

- The speed change factor, which is based on a change from the base-case average speed.

- The day and night factors, which are estimated for tactics outside the DSS.

Methodology

The discussion in this subsection is technical and is provided for completeness.

Noise estimates were computed for each of the seventy-four links of a road network; base-case traffic intensity data for these links were provided by the Ministry. With these data, highway noise for passenger and freight vehicles could be modeled.

In the methodology of the noise nuisance law, for day or night period t, define the noise level N_t as

$$N_t = E_t + C_w + C_k + C_r + D_a + D_l + D_b + D_m$$

where

E_t	=	noise emissions
C_w	=	corrections because of crossing with traffic lights

C_k = corrections because of reflection caused by buildings at the other side of the road

C_r = corrections because of type of pavement

D_a = damping because of distance

D_l = damping because of air

D_b = damping because of earth

D_m = damping because of weather

The representative noise level is defined as

$$\overline{N} = max\left(N_{day}, N_{night} + 10\right)$$

where the added 10 dB(A) for night time acknowledges a lower acceptable noise threshold for that period. The PACE-FORWARD study currently uses $C_w = C_k = C_r = 0$.

In the formulas for the remaining terms, there are four vehicle types j:

- Type 1: light vehicles, including passenger cars, vans, and trucks with four wheels.

- Type 2: light trucks, including buses and trucks with two axles and four rear wheels.

- Type 3: heavy trucks, including trucks with three or more axles, trucks with trailers, and tractors with trailers.

- Type 4: motorcycles.

The formulas for the remaining terms are as follows:

$$E_t = 10\log\sum_j 10^{E_{jt}/10}$$

$$E_{jt} = \alpha_j + \beta_j V_{jt} - 10\log V_{jt} + 10\log Q_{jt}$$

The values for α_j, β_j, and V_{jt} are given in Table 9.1. For vehicle type j during time period t, V_{jt} is average speed (in kilometers/hour), and Q_{jt} is average intensity (in vehicles/hour), the data being obtained from the Ministry for seventy-four road links (Bekkers, 1994).

Table 9.1

Parameters for the Noise Model

Vehicle Type j	α_j	β_j	V_{jt} (km/h)[a]
Light vehicles (1)	51.2	0.21	95/95
Light trucks (2)	68.4	0.09	89/89
Heavy trucks (3)	76.2	0.03	85/85
Motorcycles (4)	62.7	0.19	95/95

SOURCE: Ministry of Housing, Physical Planning, and Environment, 1981, except for velocities V_{jt}.

[a]Time t: day or night.

Continuing,

$$D_a = 10 \log a$$

$$D_l = 0.035 a^{0.75}$$

$$D_b = B\left(2 + 4(1 - e^{-0.04a})(e^{-0.65h_w} + e^{-0.65(h_r + 0.75)})\right)$$

$$D_m = 3.5(1 - e^{-0.04a/(h_w + h_r + 0.75)})$$

where a is the shortest distance between the observation point and the source (middle of lane); h_w is the height of the observation point from ground level (PACE-FORWARD assumes to it be 0 meters); h_r is the height of the road from ground level (PACE-FORWARD assumes it to be 0 meters); B is the firmness factor of the earth—0 for grass, and 1 for brick pavement, concrete, etc. (PACE-FORWARD assumes it to be 0.5).

The noise nuisance law model estimates noise as a function of distance from the highway. It is necessary to solve these nonlinear equations to obtain the minimum distance at which noise falls to a certain level. The PACE-FORWARD noise model finds an approximate solution by using curve fitting methods.

10. The Model for Macroeconomic Impacts

Some of the tactics considered in the FORWARD study could have wide and diverse ramifications in sectors of the Dutch economy other than transport. Some tactics could also have ramifications in the international arena, possibly affecting the relative economic position of the Netherlands vis-à-vis its neighbors.

Effect of Transport Sector on Other Economic Sectors

The Dutch firm NEI provided elasticity estimates for national employment and value added with respect to physical distribution costs for each of the ten (one-digit NSTR) commodity classes (see Table 10.1). That is, instead of results being shown by the sectors of the economy, they are shown by the commodity classes transported for those sectors.

The PACE-FORWARD macroeconomic impacts are measured in percent change of value added and employment with respect to the base case for the scenario

Table 10.1

Price Elasticities and Share of Distribution Costs, by Commodity Class

NSTR Commodity Class		Labor Elasticity	Value-Added Elasticity	Transport Share in Physical Distribution Costs (%)
0	Agricultural products and live animals	–0.01374	–0.01365	39.00
1	Foodstuffs and animal fodder	–0.11	–0.15	43.70
2	Solid mineral fuels[a]	–0.00135	–0.00197	47.00
3	Oil products[a]	–0.00135	–0.00197	47.00
4	Ores and metal waste	–0.00135	–0.00197	57.50
5	Metal products	–0.06094	–0.08325	56.50
6	Crude and manufactured minerals, building materials	–0.02261	–0.0254	54.30
7	Fertilizers	–0.00961	–0.01871	75.00
8	Chemicals	–0.19597	–0.31613	61.70
9	Other goods and products	–0.7502	–0.64626	39.00

SOURCE: Bozuwa, 1994b.

[a]NEI lacked the data needed to estimate the elasticities for NSTRs 2 and 3. Because these NSTRs refer to raw materials, their elasticities are most likely small. NEI thus assumed these elasticities to be the same as those of NSTR 4.

selected by the user. Thus, if the European renaissance scenario is being investigated, the PACE-FORWARD cost model computes the change in transport cost of a tactic with respect to the base case (i.e., no tactics) for each of the ten commodity classes. The percent change in physical distribution costs is then obtained by applying the share of transport in the physical distribution costs, as given in Table 10.1. It is then possible to use the elasticities in that table to obtain the percent change of value added and employment. Figure 10.1 gives the results for a sample tactic.

To obtain a single aggregate measure across all commodity classes, an overall measure is computed as the weighted sum of the percent change of value added or employment, where the weights are the fraction of tonne-kilometers attributable to each commodity type.

Along with the cost estimates it produces for the categories shown in Figure 5.1, the cost model also produces cost estimates for each of the ten commodity classes for the freight transport flows implied by the selected scenario and mode shift assumptions. These costs, together with others, are the inputs to the macroeconomic impact model.[1]

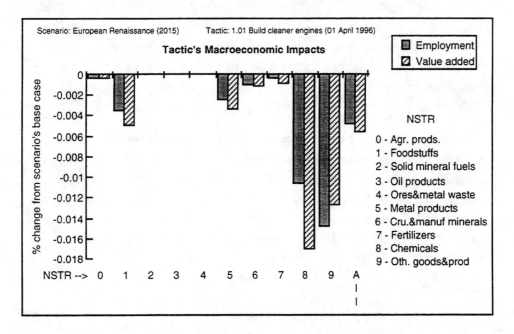

Figure 10.1—Macroeconomic Impacts for a Tactic

---

[1]The other costs associated with a tactic are normally prorated to the ten commodity classes on the basis of the tactic's tonne-kilometers in the commodity classes.

Macroeconomic Impact on Transport Sector

Of particular interest to the FORWARD study was the macroeconomic impact of tactics on the transport sector. Following NEI's suggestions, PACE-FORWARD computes an estimate of the percent change in employment in the transport sector as the percent change in tonne-kilometers adjusted by estimates of the physical productivity of labor by mode and year (see Table 10.2).

A sample display of the employment impact on the transport sector is shown in Figure 10.2. This impact can also be taken as a proxy for the percent change in value added for the transport sector.

The tonne-kilometers by various categories are the inputs to the macroeconomic impact model. To be consistent with the categories used for the physical productivity of labor (Table 10.2), the tonne-kilometers passed to this model are grouped by mode and by national or international transport.

The Macroeconomic Impact Model in Perspective

The present formulation of the macroeconomic impact model uses commodity classes as substitutes for economic sectors. To perform a more comprehensive analysis of the tactics, one needs to assess their impact on households and the government. This might be accomplished by using a more detailed cost model that tracks the cost burden shifts from households or business to government and vice versa.

Another area identified as important in the macroeconomic world is that of market share. Any tactic that affects only domestic transporters may put them at a disadvantage vis-à-vis foreign transporters. A related issue is that of port competition. The Ministry contracted with the Dutch firm NEI to try to model this area. Their results (Blok and van der Weijde, 1994) were available too late for the FORWARD study to make use of them in the PACE-FORWARD DSS.

Table 10.2

**Physical Productivity of Labor, by Transport Mode
(million tonne-kilometers per job)**

Year and Area	Road	Inland Waterway	Rail
1986 National	0.136	1.636	0.786
1986 International	1.18	4.639	0.733
2015 National	0.169	1.636	0.865
2015 International	1.887	5.614	1.027

SOURCE: Bozuwa, 1994c.

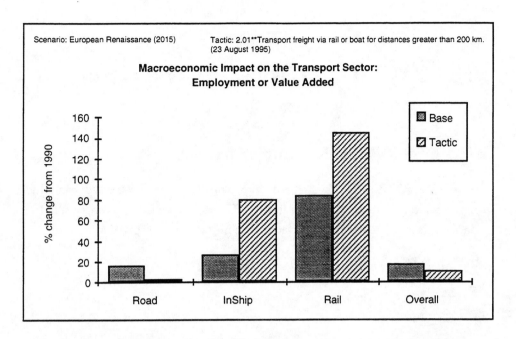

Figure 10.2—Macroeconomic Impact on the Transport Sector: Employment

11. PACE-FORWARD in Perspective

The DSS Role in the Policy Analysis

The PACE-FORWARD DSS succeeds in providing a logical framework in which to assess and compare numerous tactics affecting Dutch freight transport at the national level. The effects of the tactics are measured in terms of

- Air-pollutant emissions
- Safety
- Congestion
- Noise
- Cost
- Macroeconomic impacts

Because the DSS is implemented on a number of spreadsheets, analysts can track results from an aggregate measure to one with more detail. This can show the relative contributions of a tactic's impacts for a number of categories:[1]

- Road versus rail versus inland waterway transport
- Freight versus passenger transport
- National versus international transport

And within these categories, one can find the relative contributions by

- Geographic region
- Commodity class

There is value in having a research group apply the same assessment methodology to a large number of tactics: reproducibility of results and equal treatment of the tactics can be achieved. Describing the methodology and formalizing it into the models of the DSS allowed the reproducibility of results

---

[1]Exceptions in coverage occur for some cases. For example, the PACE-FORWARD DSS presently does not have a noise or safety model for the rail or inland waterway transport modes.

required by the scientific method. And the equal treatment of the tactics could aid the stakeholders involved in selecting tactics for implementation.

Although the measures of tactic impacts are displayed by the DSS in separate charts, they can be used as inputs in a tactic ranking scheme that incorporates the relative priorities of the stakeholders in freight transport (see Hillestad et al., 1996). In the FORWARD study, which dealt with many tactics, the separate impact measures were sufficient for discarding the nonpromising tactics, making the task of screening the tactics more manageable.

Analysis as a Complement to the DSS Results

Like any DSS, PACE-FORWARD cannot capture all facets of the world it represents, nor can it overcome the fact that decisions based on its results do not take into consideration areas either not covered or not covered adequately by the models. However, we felt that assessing over one hundred tactics was so challenging a task that it should be thought of as a best attempt at screening and assessing those tactics within the study's limited time and resources.

Because of the large number of tactics involved, the related transitional implementation and political issues were explicitly left out of the FORWARD study. Any decision to pursue a specific tactic or strategy would require a more in-depth assessment and more careful attention to implementation and political issues. For example, although a tactic's total net cost may be negligible, a shift of the cost burden (e.g., from business to individuals, from business to government, or vice versa) may be involved. A change such as this clearly has political ramifications that require more detailed study before an implementation decision is made.

The DSS Implementation

The Excel spreadsheet environment proved to be well suited for policy analysis. It provided the ability to link various spreadsheet models and major databases, thereby allowing us to integrate the various models of the DSS. This linkage capability facilitates incremental development of modular components and prototyping, which are major requirements of an environment that keeps growing, in both models and databases, as it attempts to cover more tactics. PACE-FORWARD's practical tactic- and model-selection mechanism made full use of this linkage capability in providing full data base access to the models.

The programmable GUI of the spreadsheet environment makes the DSS accessible to many analysts. Since PACE-FORWARD was designed to support the policy analysis in the FORWARD study, the design emphasis was on functionality, which means that relatively little time was spent on GUI development or maintainability. Nevertheless, the GUI proved adequate for the study analysts in both the United States and the Netherlands.

The varied programmable computational tools of a spreadsheet environment can be used to automate repetitive and computationally intensive tasks. For PACE-FORWARD, this means that a large number of transport tactics can be evaluated, since the analyst, freed from concentrating on repetitive tasks, can focus on conceptual challenges and on maintaining a top-level decision-maker's perspective.

Suggested Areas for Future Work

The models in PACE-FORWARD use mainly the methodology of existing Dutch models; exceptions to this are the congestion model, which is new, and the NEI macroeconomic effects model, which was developed concurrently with—but separately from—the FORWARD study. The verification and validation of PACE-FORWARD were carried out to some extent during the FORWARD study, the careful scrutiny of the tactic results being a major contributor. This validation process is useful and should proceed at some level.

Given that the models may lead to the selection or exclusion of a given tactic, it would not be surprising for them to be challenged or at least subjected to greater scrutiny. If they are, the end result could be enhanced or refined models, or even the replacement of some models by others.

Some models in the PACE-FORWARD DSS could probably be improved or just refined. For example, the cost and macroeconomic models need to be able to identify impact areas affecting households and government so that a better assessment can be made of the shifts in cost burdens resulting from a tactic.

Some effort was made to rank tactics on a cost-effectiveness basis that incorporated stakeholder priorities. However, the area of multiple-criteria decision making needs to be revisited, especially in cases where costs could be separated into costs to households, to business, and to government.

As the DSS is used to evaluate more tactics, the level of resolution of its models should be reassessed. Changes in this area could enhance its ability to represent additional tactics and/or affect the speed at which it executes the models (see the

Appendix for DSS speed statistics). For example, reorganizing the DSS models to put greater emphasis on the network representation of the three modes of transport might give the DSS greater accuracy or at least enable it to provide statistics by network link.

The DSS database management system could be enhanced to take advantage of the new data analysis capabilities, such as pivot tables, available in Excel version 5 (Microsoft Corporation, 1994).

The data estimates in Dutch government and other data sources could be improved. (Any data improvements would probably have a greater effect on the results than the models would.) In the FORWARD study, a multidisciplinary team of researchers primarily used previous studies to obtain or derive the model parameters for the base case and the tactics. As better parameter estimates become available, they should be incorporated into the database of tactics.

Finally, PACE-FORWARD's implementation could be enhanced to make it more maintainable and to facilitate its documentation, both of which should also make it accessible to more analysts. Little effort was dedicated to maintainability and documentation, because PACE-FORWARD was built primarily to support the FORWARD study and export of the DSS was not a requirement. The study needs for maintainability and for documentation and consultation were fulfilled mainly by the DSS designer and developer.

Appendix

Implementation Statistics for the PACE-FORWARD DSS

The PACE-FORWARD implementation has the following major characteristics:

- Approximately 2600 lines of (U.S.) Excel 4 macros (two files)
- Sixty-two files, most with formulas, occupying 9.6 megabytes of storage
- Eleven dialog boxes
- Twenty chart types
- Six major impact models

Once the definition of a tactic is entered into the DSS data base and a scenario is selected, about 100 seconds of elapsed time are needed to run all the impact models on a Macintosh Quadra 800 computer with 12 megabytes of RAM and Macintosh operating system 7.1.

Bibliography

Bekkers, J., "Hourly Traffic Intensities for 1991; Road Capacities for 1991; Congestion Data for 1990-1992; Road Safety Data for 1986–1991," Ministry of Transport, Public Works, and Water Management: Transport Research Centre, Rotterdam, March 1994.

Blok, P.M., and I. van der Weijde, *Uitvlaggen wegvervoeractiviteiten: kwalitatieve beschouwing en kwantitatieve aanzet; Deelonderzoek in kader van ontwikkeling FORWARD model*, Netherlands Economic Institute, Rotterdam, 1994.

Blok, P.M., et al., *Verkennend onderzoek: Verbeteringen efficiency in het goederenvervoer: Trends + maatregelen (Exploratory Research: Improving Efficiency in Freight Transport: Trends and Measures)*, YD/T1840, Netherlands Economic Institute, Rotterdam, July 27, 1992.

Blok, P.M., et al., *Het Trendbreukscenario in economisch perspectief*, YD/T1857, Netherlands Economic Institute, Rotterdam, July 5, 1993.

Blok, P.M., et al., *De lasten van de kosten, effecten van doorberekening van infrastructuur- en externe kosten aan het goederenvervoer*, GIN/YD/T2225, Netherlands Economic Institute, Rotterdam, December 1993.

Bozuwa, J., Netherlands Economic Institute, memorandum to FORWARD Team RAND/EAC, April 22, 1994a.

Bozuwa, J., Netherlands Economic Institute, memorandum to Odette van de Riet, May 5, 1994b.

Bozuwa, J., Netherlands Economic Institute, memorandum to Odette van de Riet, June 8, 1994c.

Bozuwa, J., Netherlands Economic Institute, memorandum to Odette van de Riet, June 30, 1994d.

CBS (Central Bureau of Statistics), *Het bezit en gebruik van de bedrijfsvoertuigen 1989 (Ownership and use of Commercial Motor Vehicles, 1989)*, CBS, Voorburg/Heerlen, 1990.

CBS, *Nationale Rekeningen: 1990*, CBS-Publications, The Hague, 1991.

CBS, *Statistical Yearbook of the Netherlands, 1992*, CBS-Publications, The Hague, 1992a.

CBS, *Luchtverontreiniging; emissies door wegverkeer 1980–1990*, SDU Publishers, The Hague, 1992b.

CPB (Central Planning Bureau), *Nederland in drievoud; Een scenariostudie van de Nederlandse economie: 1990–2015*, The Hague, September 1992.

DHV Raadgevend Ingenieursbureau BV, *Akoestisch ruimtebeslag van het primarie wegennet in Nederland*, Ministry of Transport, Public Works, and Water Management, Rijkswaterstaat, Dienst Weg- Waterbouwkunde, the Netherlands, June 1988.

Drie, M. van, Ministry of Transport, Public Works, and Water Management, Transport Research Centre, memorandum to E. Baarspul, September 30, 1994.

Hillestad, R.J., et al., *FORWARD—Freight Options for Road, Water, and Rail for the Dutch: Final Report*, MR-736-EAC/VW, RAND, 1996.

Hu, T.C., *Integer Programming and Network Flows*, Addison-Wesley Publishing Company, Reading, Massachusetts, 1969.

Klein, J.A.P., *Statistische onderzoekingen, luchtverontreiniging, emissies door wegverkeer, methodiek vaststelling emissiefactoren*, CBS, The Hague, 1993.

Knight-Wendling Consultant BV, *Macro-economische en maatschappelijke kosten-baten analyse van de Betuweroute tabellen, eindrapport*, November 1992.

McKinsey and Company, *Economische aantrekkelijkheid goederenvervoer per spoor; Samenvattende rapportage*, Ministry of Transport, Public Works, and Water Management, The Hague, September 1992.

Microsoft Corporation, *Microsoft Excel: User's Guide, Version 4*, Redmond, Washington, 1992.

Microsoft Corporation, *Microsoft Excel: User's Guide, Version 5*, Redmond, Washington, 1994.

Ministry of Housing, Physical Planning, and Environment, *Berekening van wegverkeersgeluid; Een toelichting op de standaard-rekenmethode I uit het reken- en meetvoorschrift verkeerslawaai artikel 102 wet geluidshinder*, The Hague, 1981.

Ministry of Housing, Physical Planning and Environment, *Reken- en meetvoorschrift verkeerslawaai; Regeling als bedoeld in artikel 102, eerste en tweede lid, van de wet geluidshinder*, Staatsuitgeverij, The Hague, 1981.

NEA, *The Transport of Goods by Road and Its Environment in the Europe of Tomorrow*, Rijswijk, the Netherlands, March 1992a.

NEA, *Euret 2.1: Country Report: The Netherlands*, Rijswijk, the Netherlands, November 1992b.

NEA, "Databases for the TEM model," Rijswijk, the Netherlands, February 1993a.

NEA, *Filekosten op het Nederlandse hoofdwegennet in 1991 en 1992*, Rijswijk, the Netherlands, April 1993b.

Oum, T.H., W.G. Waters II, and J-S Yong, "Concepts of Price-Elasticities of Transport Demand and Recent Empirical Estimates," *Journal of Transport Economics and Policy*, 23(2), 1989.

Tavasszy, L.A., *Characteristics and Capabilities of Dutch Freight Transportation Systems Models*, MR-382-EAC/VW, RAND, 1994.

Turban, E., *Decision Support and Expert System: Managerial Perspectives*, Macmillan Publishing Co., New York, 1988.

van Minnen, J., *Analyse van de verkeersonveiligheid van sware voertuigen (Analysis of the Traffic Safety of Heavy Vehicles)*, SWOV (Institute for Scientific Research on Traffic Safety), Leidschendam, 1992.